Olympia On-Time!

(a story about timeliness)

by Wade Gugino

For Tod, whose character is an example to all of us.

Artists & Musicians:

Wade Gugino
Story, Pencil, Ink,
Layout, Color, Lyrics

Abram Siegel
Music Development
& Editing

Eva Marie Gugino
Story Narration &
Digital Audio

ISBN 978-0-9894829-0-5   Printed in the United States.

Special thanks to the West Michigan Character Council and the Community
Foundation of the Holland & Zeeland Area for their development support.

All characters, story, titles and layout are © and ™ Googenius, LLC. All rights reserved. No part of this publication may be reproduced in whole or in part, or stored in a retrieval system, or transmitted in any form or by any means, electronic, mechanical, photocopying, recording or otherwise without written permission of the publisher. For information regarding permission, contact info@Googenius.com.

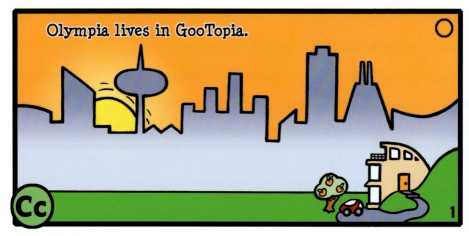

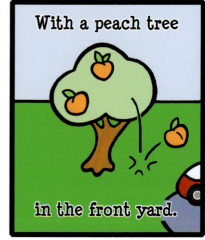

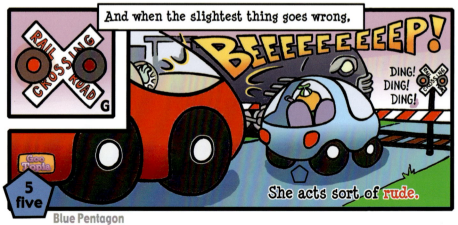

When she gets to work it's late, late, late,

So she starts making big excuses.

But her boss knows Olympia's problem really is the choices that she chooses.

Purple Hexagon

What Olympia doesn't understand, Is that when she shows up late and angry,

She makes everyone else's life just a little crazy.

Maroon Octagon

Black Half-Circle

Drawing on Character

Drawing helps you remember what you learn. Try drawing Olympia step by step with an adult or on your own.
Draw the gray parts, then move to the next step and do the same until you're done.

For more drawing instructions and to download coloring pages, visit www.GooGuysAndGals.com

Glossary:

Passive Solar Home: A house that is built to collect and hold heat from the sun's light to keep it warm in the winter, and reflect the sun's light to keep it cool in summer.

Irate: is another word for Angry. It's a forceful kind of anger, usually brought on by something that irritates you. Olympia's alarm clock irritates her to the point of becoming irate.

Berserk: is another word for Crazy. Olympia got so angry when things weren't working the way she wanted, that she started to act a little bit crazy. You can go berserk when you're happy, too!

Production Line: Factory workers will often work together in a line. Olympia does her part making the product, then passes it down the line to other workers until the product is finished.

Crummy: means Yucky or Unpleasant. When Olympia's a little sick she says, "I feel kind of crummy." When she has a bad day, she sighs and says, "Well that was a pretty crummy day."

Shift: Some jobs are done all day and night. One set of workers can't work all that time, but groups of workers can. The time that Olympia's group comes in to work is called their Shift.

For more great vocabulary words visit www.GooGuysAndGals.com

Character Toon-Up:

How can YOU learn to be On-Time, and help your family be On-Time?

- DO what you are asked to do, and DO IT RIGHT AWAY when you are asked.

- If you have homework or a job to do, DON'T WAIT to start it, GET GOING RIGHT AWAY.

- Get ready to go places and do things WITHOUT GETTING DISTRACTED. Being ready helps everyone.

- LISTEN to what people are saying to you so that YOU KNOW WHAT YOU NEED TO DO when it's time to do it.

Learn more ways to Toon-Up your character at
www.GooGuysAndGals.com!

Sound Thinking!

Get your body moving with Olympia! Movement helps your brain hold on to the information you've learned. Go ahead...Shake it! Twirl it! Rock it! Learn it! And then listen to the story all over again!

ON THE CD:
1. Be On-Time Olympia Song
2. Olympia On-Time Story Narration

Bonus Audio
1. Spanish Version Narration
2. Be On-Time Olympia Instrumental
3. GooSmart Vocabulary Narration

Purchase the CD or download the digital story and song at www.GooGuysAndGals.com

Music Layout: Abram Siegel
Lyrics and Vocals: Wade Gugino
Story Narration: Eva Marie Gugino
Spanish Narration: Martha Boeve

Welcome to GooTopia®™

Goo Guys & Gals Graphic Readers®™ are designed to help young children take an interest in reading, prepare them to start school on the right foot, and begin a lifelong awareness of character values...three of the most important elements of learning and future success...all wrapped up in visual, fun stories that grow with little minds!

More Goo Guys & Gals Coming Soon:

Rolando Responsible | Harrison Humble | Captain Carlos Courage | Esmeralda Enthusiastic | Jasper Joyful | Lord Linus the Loyal | Norbert Noble

Development of Olympia On-Time was made possible by grants from:

A Googenius Product. For more information on all our products, visit www.Googenius.com.

$5.00
ISBN 978-0-9894829-0-5
50500>

9 780989 482905